DC
COMICS™

# BATMOBILES
## AND
# BATCYCLES

### THE ENGINEERING BEHIND
### BATMAN'S VEHICLES

BY TAMMY ENZ

BATMAN CREATED BY
BOB KANE

## BATMAN
## SCIENCE™

CAPSTONE PRESS
a capstone imprint

Published by Capstone Press in 2014
A Capstone Imprint
1710 Roe Crest Drive
North Mankato, Minnesota 56003
www.capstonepub.com

**Library of Congress Cataloging-in-Publication Data**
Cataloging-in-publication information is on file with the Library of Congress.
ISBN 978-1-4765-3940-9 (library binding)
ISBN 978-1-4765-5208-8 (paperback)

Summary: Explores the real-world science and engineering connections to the features in Batman's road vehicles.

**Editorial Credits**
Editor: Christopher L. Harbo
Designer: Veronica Scott
Production Specialist: Kathy McColley

**Photo Credits**
Alamy: A. T. Willett, 15, ZUMA Press/Nancy Kaszerman, 17; AP Images: Mel Evans, 11 (bottom); Dreamstime: Editor77, 13; Getty Images: Bloomberg, 25; Newscom: AFP/Getty Images/Karen Bleier, 23, AFP/Getty Images/Toshifumi Kitamura, 11 (top), picture-alliance/dpa/Boris Roessler, 26, WENN. com, 21 (bottom), ZUMA Press/Sutton Motorsports, 9, ZUMA Press/UPPA, 8-9; Shutterstock: Eugene Chernetsov, 6; U.S. Air Force photo by Master Sgt. Jeremy Lock, 12, Staff Sgt. Joseph Swafford Jr., 16, Staff Sgt. Bennie J. Davis III, 14; U.S. Army photo by Spc. Kayla Benson, 18, Spc. Ryan A. Cleary, 27; U.S. Marine Corps photo by Lance Cpl. Joey Chavez, 29; U.S. Navy photo, 7 (bottom), PO2 Robert J. Whelan, 28; U.S. Secret Service, 19; Wikimedia: IFCAR, 7 (top), BMK, 21 (top)

Design Elements: Shutterstock: BiterBig, ClickHere, Jason Winter

Printed in the United States of America in Stevens Point, Wisconsin.
009940R

# TABLE OF CONTENTS

INTRODUCTION
SUPER HERO WHEELS ..................................................................4

CHAPTER 1
PERFORMANCE STANDARDS ...................................................... 6

CHAPTER 2
TRICKS OF THE TRADE............................................................. 12

CHAPTER 3
SUPERSTRONG AND SECURE ..................................................... 18

CHAPTER 4
DRIVER INTERFACE ................................................................. 22

CHAPTER 5
ENGAGING THE ENEMY ............................................................. 26

GLOSSARY ............................................................................... 30

READ MORE ............................................................................. 31

INTERNET SITES........................................................................ 31

INDEX ..................................................................................... 32

# SUPER HERO WHEELS

When it comes to cool vehicles, the Batcave is well-stocked. Throughout his crime-fighting history, the Caped Crusader has developed an eye-popping collection of Batmobiles and Batcycles. His wheels range from sporty cars to stout military-type vehicles. In fact, some stories show Batman owning a whole fleet of Batmobiles. And in each one, amazing gadgets and awesome power are standard features. From high-tech engines to bulletproof tires, Batman's vehicles make your jaw drop. But are their features pure science fiction?

Believe it or not, most of the cutting-edge technology in Batman's road vehicles exists in real life. Without a doubt, real engineering feats have inspired Batman's vehicles. But some real-world engineering actually matches the awesome features in the Batmobile. Need proof? Get ready to explore the science and engineering behind the Dark Knight's Batmobiles and Batcycles.

# CHAPTER 1

# PERFORMANCE STANDARDS

Batman depends on his road vehicles. Powerful engines and precise steering ensure that no enemy is a match for the Batmobile or the Batcycle. But Batman's advanced technologies are not all super hero fiction.

## POWER BOOSTS

Chasing down Gotham City's super-villains requires maximum power from Batman's vehicles. To achieve it, he experiments with a variety of high-tech engines. These engines include **turbochargers** and **atomic energy**. In the real world airplanes have used turbocharged engines since the early 1900s. These engines increase power. They pump an extra dose of an air-gas mixture into the engine's cylinders. The extra air-gas produces more power when burned. Turbocharged engines boost the power of regular engines by 30 to 40 percent.

turbocharger

The 1962 Oldsmobile Jetfire was one of the first cars to use a turbocharger. But early turbocharged car engines were unreliable. Carmakers stopped making them until high gas prices and better engineering brought them back. Today turbocharging gives small cars more power and better gas mileage.

The BMW 328i sedan is one of many modern cars that boasts a turbocharged engine.

# ATOMIC ENERGY

Turbochargers are cool, but what about atomic engines? In 1954 the USS *Nautilus* became the first submarine to use an atomic engine. This engine allowed the sub to stay underwater longer than any previous submarine. In 1958 the *Nautilus* became the first known vessel to reach the North Pole. It traveled under the arctic ice to get there.

**turbocharger**—a system that forces air through an engine to make a car go faster

**atomic energy**—energy produced by splitting the atom

# RAPID ACCELERATION

Flame-releasing power bursts are signature moves of the Batmobile and the Batcycle. Rocket thrusters give Batman fast starts and rapid **acceleration**. They always leave the bad guys eating dust.

Normal cars don't have rocket thrusters, but some experimental cars do. One such vehicle is the British rocket-propelled Thrust Supersonic Car (SSC). It was built with two 20,000-pound (9,100-kilogram) Rolls-Royce Spey engines. These huge engines were originally designed for jet planes.

**acceleration**—the change in speed of a moving body

On October 15, 1997, ThrustSSC proved just how fast it could go. British fighter pilot Andy Green tested the car in the Black Rock Desert in Nevada. He reached 763 miles (1,228 kilometers) per hour. ThrustSSC set the world record as the fastest land vehicle on Earth. It also became the first car to break the speed of sound.

ThrustSSC

## FACT:

ENGINEER JAMES WATTS (1736–1819) COINED THE TERM HORSEPOWER. IT MEASURES AN ENGINE'S POWER BY COMPARING IT TO THE AMOUNT OF WORK A DRAFT HORSE CAN DO.

# BLOODHOUND SSC

Bloodhound SSC is another British built rocket car. It is designed to go even faster than ThrustSSC. It hopes to use a jet engine to reach about 230 miles (370 km) per hour. Then it will fire a rocket to reach more than 1,000 miles (1,600 km) per hour. At full speed, the engine will run at about 80,000 horsepower. That's equal to the power of 95 Formula One race cars.

HAMPSON

Bloodhound SSC

# TIGHT CORNERING

In car chases, taking corners with speed is key. To keep Batman in the hunt, the Batmobile and Batcycle sometimes use unique **axle** and wheel designs. These features help his vehicles make extremely tight corners and 360-degree turns.

To find innovative cornering systems in the real world, look no further than Bimota in Italy. The motorcycle company's Tesi 3D uses hub-centered steering. This motorcycle looks different because it doesn't have a fork connected to its front wheel. Instead, horizontal bars extend from the side of the bike. These bars push and pull the wheel when the handlebars turn. This mechanism allows the wheel to rotate more freely on its axle. The Tesi 3D gives riders quicker, steadier turns than traditional motorcycles.

The Tesi 3D doesn't have a traditional fork connected to the front wheels.

The Airtrax Sidewinder 3000's angled rollers make tight turns.

Motorcycles aren't the only cool rides with unique wheels. The wheels on the Airtrax Sidewinder 3000 will make you do a double take. This **omnidirectional** forklift uses a circular set of angled rollers as wheels. When in motion, these rollers act like a ball. They allow the forklift to move in any direction—even sideways. In packed warehouses the Sidewinder easily glides through tight spaces.

**axle**—a rod in the center of a wheel, around which the wheel turns
**omnidirectional**—moving in all directions

You've experienced the brawn of the Batmobile and Batcycle. But their smart technologies really set them apart from other vehicles. With stealth mode, ejection seats, and other capabilities, there's almost nothing these vehicles can't do.

# STEALTH MODE

The chase is on. But with enemies on its tail, the Batmobile suddenly disappears. Where did it go? With its lights off and a quiet engine, the Batmobile has entered stealth mode.

The F-22 Raptor's body shape and covering help it stay hidden from enemy radar.

Hiding in plain sight has been a military goal for decades. Although complete invisibility isn't possible, some aircraft can disappear from enemy **radar**. Radar systems send out bursts of radio energy. When it hits an object, the energy bounces back and shows the object's location. Absorbing or deflecting radar signals hides an object's location.

In the 1980s the U.S. military unveiled the first stealth aircraft. The F-117A fighter jet's sharp edges and angles reflected radar at odd angles. Its surface was also coated with a top-secret radar absorbent material (RAM). These technologies made the plane look like a small bird on radar screens. The military retired the F-117A in 2008, but other stealth aircraft have taken its place. These stealth flyers include the B-2 Spirit, F-22 Raptor, and F-35 Lightning.

## TOO STEALTHY?

Stealth mode has its drawbacks. Electric and hybrid car engines make almost no noise. Their silence is dangerous for bikers and walkers who don't hear them coming. In 2013 the U.S. National Highway Traffic Safety Administration (NHTSA) proposed a new rule. It would require that these vehicles add noisemakers to their engines.

**stealth**—having the ability to move secretly

**radar**—an electronic device that uses radio waves to determine the location of an object such as a flying airplane

# EJECTION SEAT

The Batmobile crashes through the guardrail and careens off the edge of a bridge. The vehicle plunges toward the river below. Is it game over for Batman? Not likely. The Batmobile's ejection seat ensures his survival.

Ejection seats are a common real-world technology in aircraft. They have been standard equipment in most military aircraft since World War II (1939–1945). These days ejection seats are one of the most complicated systems on an aircraft. They have thousands of parts. Each part must work flawlessly to save a pilot's life.

An Air Force pilot ejects from a fighter jet after guiding it safely away from an air show crowd.

The entire ejection sequence happens in just four action-packed seconds. In an emergency a pilot pulls a handle. Explosive bolts then blast off the cockpit canopy. A rocket motor launches the seat up to 200 feet (61 meters) above the plane. When the pilot is safely away from the plane, a small parachute opens. As the pilot falls, a sensor tracks his or her **altitude**. When a safe altitude is reached, the main parachute opens. At the same time, a motor blasts the ejection seat away from the pilot. The pilot then floats to the ground.

## ACES II

U.S. Air Force planes use Advanced Concept Ejection Seats (ACES II). These "smart seats" decide when to release parachutes. They also sense when the seat is tumbling out of control. The seats use small rockets to counteract the tumbling forces.

### FACT:

EJECTION SEATS HAVE BEEN SUCCESSFULLY USED IN AIRCRAFT FLYING AT SPEEDS UP TO 800 MILES (1,287 KM) PER HOUR.

altitude—how high a place is above sea level

# MULTI-FUNCTION

It's a car. It's a plane. It's a boat. No, it's all three! Batman's vehicles are way more than what they seem. They can easily change function to perform where the action takes them.

Vehicles that can transition between environments have been around for ages. An **amphibious** tug called the Alligator helped loggers haul cargo over land and water in the 1880s. In 1937 the Waterman Aerobile took to the skies as the first flying car. But time-consuming transitions made these early vehicles impractical.

Modern vehicles perform quick changes when they transition. The Gibbs Humdinga changes from land vehicle to watercraft in as little as five seconds. Its **suspension** uses sensors to detect when water is deep enough to float. Then the Humdinga's wheels and brakes fold up into its body. A supercharged V-8 engine powers the vehicle on land. Twin jets push it through the water. It can travel more than 30 miles (48 km) per hour on water. It reaches highway speeds on land.

The wheels of a Gibbs Humdinga peek out of the water as it glides across a marina.

Going from land to water is one thing. But what about leaving the open road for the clear blue sky? The Terrafugia Transition is a car with folding wings. On land it drives like a regular car and fits in a garage. To take flight, the Terrafugia unfolds its wings and cruises at about 105 miles (169 km) per hour. It can fly up to 490 miles (789 km) on a single tank of gas.

The Terrafugia Transition's folding wings allow it to drive down the road like a car.

**amphibious**—able to work on land or water

**suspension**—the system of springs and shock absorbers that absorbs a car's up-and-down movements

17

# CHAPTER 3

# SUPERSTRONG AND SECURE

Few vehicles have safety features that match the Batmobile's or Batcycle's. No disaster or explosion slows these vehicles down. Their armored bodies and bulletproof tires keep them rolling.

## BULLETPROOF AND EXPLOSION-PROOF BODIES

The Batmobile is one of the toughest cars ever designed. It deflects bullets. It blasts through walls of flames. But are real-world vehicles able to handle these conditions?

Armored trucks and military vehicles use bulletproof and explosion-proof technology. They are outfitted with **ceramic** plates, Kevlar fabric, and bulletproof glass.

A soldier peers through the bulletproof glass of a heavily armored Humvee gun turret.

The ceramic plates in armored trucks and military Humvees aren't made out of the same ceramic as coffee mugs. These slabs of baked boron carbide are so hard they're sometimes called "black diamond." Bullets shatter when they hit these slabs. Ceramic plates are often layered with reinforced plastics or fabrics. They are placed inside door panels or attached to the outside skin of military vehicles.

Kevlar fabric is also used for bulletproofing. This tightly woven fabric is similar to nylon but stronger. It is almost impossible to tear or melt. Layers of Kevlar absorb a bullet's energy to slow it down and stop it.

Windows present a unique bulletproofing challenge. Bulletproof windows are made of a **polycarbonate** layer sandwiched between regular glass. Polycarbonate is a tough plastic. A bullet breaks through the layers of regular glass, but is stopped by the polycarbonate layer.

## THE BEAST

The U.S. president's limo may be the only car that compares to the Batmobile for its armor. The president's limousine is nicknamed "The Beast." On top of body armor, it is decked out with night-vision cameras and Kevlar tires. For extra protection, the limo has its own oxygen supply. It also has a backup blood supply for the president.

ceramic—having to do with objects made out of clay
polycarbonate—a high strength, lightweight plastic

# BULLETPROOF TIRES

Dodging enemy fire and off-road driving take a toll on ordinary tires. But Batman doesn't have time for a flat. Whether using puncture-proof or **auxiliary** tires, Batman's vehicles get him to his destination every time.

In the real world, you might be riding on a set of high-tech tires without ever knowing it. Military vehicles and some passenger cars use run-flat tires. Normal tires need to be filled with air, like a balloon. The air pressure inside the tire holds up the weight of the car. When these tires puncture, they lose air and can't be driven. Run-flat tires have stiff sidewalls to support the weight of the car. Even without air, a run-flat tire can be driven up to 100 miles (161 km).

Auxiliary supported tires are another type of high-tech tire. They are built like a tire inside a tire. Their solid inner ring carries the weight of the vehicle if the outer tire blows out. Michelin's PAX auxiliary tire can run flat for up to 125 miles (200 km) at 55 miles (89 km) per hour.

inner ring

The solid inner ring supports an auxiliary tire in the event of a flat.

# HONEYCOMB TIRES

The U.S. military asked engineers to come up with a tire design that doesn't use air at all. Resilient Technologies and the University of Wisconsin—Madison answered this engineering challenge. They designed a tire **polymer** constructed in a honeycombed pattern. This tire can withstand an explosion and still make a speedy getaway.

**auxiliary**—helping, or giving extra support

**polymer**—tiny pieces of matter that are linked together; there are natural polymers and human-made polymers

Batman's vehicles are all about attitude. They talk to Batman and drive themselves. And don't even think about hiding from the Batmobile or the Batcycle. They sense everything around them.

# REMOTE DRIVE

The Batmobile's self-driving feature is a super hero's dream. Batman can call his car with a remote control. It then winds its way through Gotham City for a speedy pickup.

In the real world, Google has been testing self-driving cars since 2010. A Google car charts a course toward a programmed location. It heads out using cameras and a fast-spinning **laser** eye. These tools see traffic lights, stop signs, and other cars on the road. The car's computers react to this information. Google cars have logged more than 300,000 miles (483,000 km) of driving with no reported accidents.

Totally driverless cars are years away, but some cars already help with simple driving tasks. BMW's traffic jam assistant helps control the car in stop-and-go traffic jams. As long as the driver keeps one hand on the wheel, the car stays a constant distance from the vehicle ahead of it. The car also keeps itself in its own lane.

The sensor on the roof of a Google car helps it navigate the streets of Washington, D.C.

# SPIRIT OF BERLIN

Spirit of Berlin is a car controlled by a cell phone app. Students at a university in Berlin, Germany, developed the app to control the car's steering, braking, and acceleration. A camera placed on the car's dashboard sends video to a smartphone user. The user drives the car using the phone's touch screen.

**laser**—a thin, intense, high-energy beam of light

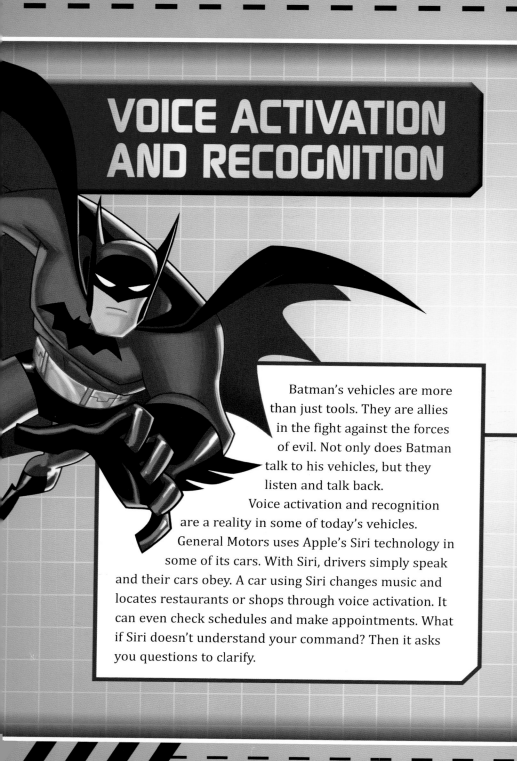

# VOICE ACTIVATION AND RECOGNITION

Batman's vehicles are more than just tools. They are allies in the fight against the forces of evil. Not only does Batman talk to his vehicles, but they listen and talk back.

Voice activation and recognition are a reality in some of today's vehicles. General Motors uses Apple's Siri technology in some of its cars. With Siri, drivers simply speak and their cars obey. A car using Siri changes music and locates restaurants or shops through voice activation. It can even check schedules and make appointments. What if Siri doesn't understand your command? Then it asks you questions to clarify.

Ford's SYNC technology recognizes and responds to the driver's voice. SYNC can tell the difference between a driver's voice and loud traffic or the radio. It learns how a driver says certain words and responds to his or her accent. With simple voice commands, SYNC helps drivers make phone calls, control music, and get traffic directions.

An attendee at a technology show tries a demonstration on a SYNC control console.

Batman's vehicles excel at tracking down notorious criminals and detecting their weapons. The Batmobile and Batcycle help foil evil schemes and defend justice at every turn. Luckily, the real world has many of Batman's defensive technologies.

# WEAPONS DETECTION SYSTEM

The villains of Gotham City will stop at nothing to rid themselves of the Caped Crusader. And they have a stash of high-powered weapons to get the job done. But the Batmobile's weapons detection system is always on alert for potential threats.

Weapons detection is a huge concern at airports around the world. Since 2006 Advanced Imaging Technology (AIT) has helped look for hidden weapons. These machines use microwaves to scan a person's body. They create an image of a person's body and locate any suspicious objects. These scanners are more sensitive than older metal detectors. They not only find metal weapons, but also **plastic explosives** and ceramic knives.

An airline passenger raises her arms as she is scanned by an AIT machine.

The military has special detectors to track and identify chemical and biological weapons. These detectors are called Biological Integrated Detection Systems (BIDS). BIDS mount to Humvees or Black Hawk helicopters. They use lasers to scan the air and detect unnatural agents. These systems quickly find chemical and biological weapons and alert soldiers to the danger.

The Ohio National Guard shows off a BIDS mounted on the back of a Humvee.

# FAST M²

Since 2008 the Department of Homeland Security has been testing a new way to find people planning to commit crimes. The Future Attribute Screening Technology Mobile Module (FAST M²) scans eye movements, heart rates, gestures, and facial expressions. Rapid heart rates and eye movements could mean a person is up to no good.

# WEAPONS

When it comes to weapons, Batman's vehicles have more under the hood than just raw firepower. In road battles, Batman always aims to disable his enemies. To accomplish this, his vehicles often use disruptive weapons such as caltrops and smoke screens.

Caltrops have been around for thousands of years. These spiky weapons made effective low-tech land mines for ancient and medieval warriors. Scattering them on roadways and across the countryside slowed down advancing armies. Caltrops injured horses and camels, and they tripped up foot soldiers.

Military and police forces still use caltrops in the form of spike strips. Spike strips are rows of metal spikes. They are laid out on a road in front of a speeding car. They puncture tires and disable getaway vehicles.

A soldier puts down a spike strip at a checkpoint in Iraq.

Smoke screens also have modern uses. Soldiers use smoke screens to hide their movements from the enemy. Some banks also use smoke screens to prevent burglaries. When robbers enter a vault, the touch of a button causes thick smoke to suddenly fill the air. When the robbers lose their bearings, they usually take off or get caught.

Soldiers crouch behind a smoke screen to conceal their movements.

# PACKED WITH TECHNOLOGY

Batman's vehicles pack in a lot of amazing technology. They command the streets of Gotham City with high-powered engines and clever weapons. But the Batmobile and Batcycle are more than just tools for a fictional super hero. Their features remind us of the science and engineering we see and use every day.

# GLOSSARY

**acceleration** (ak-sel-uh-RAY-shuhn)—the change in speed of a moving body

**altitude** (AL-ti-tood)—how high a place is above sea level

**amphibious** (am-FI-bee-uhs)—able to work on land or water

**atomic energy** (uh-TOM-ik E-nuhr-jee)—energy produced by splitting the atom

**auxiliary** (awg-ZIL-yur-ee)—helping, or giving extra support

**axle** (AK-suhl)—a rod in the center of a wheel, around which the wheel turns

**ceramic** (suh-RA-mik)—having to do with objects made out of clay

**laser** (LAY-zur)—a thin, intense, high-energy beam of light

**omnidirectional** (om-nee-duh-REK-shuhn-uhl)—moving in all directions

**plastic explosive** (PLASS-tik ek-SPLOH-siv)—a combination of a high explosive and wax

**polycarbonate** (pol-ee-CAR-buh-nayt)—a high strength, lightweight plastic

**polymer** (POL-uh-mur)—tiny pieces of matter that are linked together; there are natural polymers and human-made polymers

**radar** (RAY-dar)—an electronic device that uses radio waves to determine the location of an object such as a flying airplane

**stealth** (STELTH)—having the ability to move secretly

**suspension** (suh-SPEN-shuhn)—the system of springs and shock absorbers that absorbs a car's up-and-down movements

**turbocharger** (TUR-boh-char-juhr)—a system that forces air through an engine to make a car go faster

# READ MORE

**Colson, Rob.** *Tanks and Military Vehicles.* Ultimate Machines. New York: PowerKids Press, 2013.

**Gilpin, Daniel, and Alex Pang.** *Modern Military Aircraft.* Machines Close-up. New York: Marshall Cavendish Benchmark, 2011.

**Graham, Ian.** *Cars.* Design and Engineering for STEM. Chicago: Capstone Heinemann Library, 2013.

**Townsend, John.** *Cars and Motorcycles.* Science and Technology. Chicago: Raintree, 2012.

# INTERNET SITES

FactHound offers a safe, fun way to find Internet sites related to this book. All of the sites on FactHound have been researched by our staff.

Here's all you do:

Visit *www.facthound.com*

Type in this code: 9781476539409

# INDEX

Advanced Imaging Technology (AIT), 26
Airtrax Sidewinder 3000, 11
Alligator tug, 16
atomic energy, 6, 7

Bloodhound SSC, 9
bulletproof glass, 18, 19
bulletproof tires, 4, 18, 19, 20–21

caltrops, 28
ceramic plates, 18–19

ejection seats, 12, 14–15
electric and hybrid cars, 13

Future Attribute Screening Technology
    Mobile Module (FAST M²), 27

Gibbs Humdinga, 16
Google car, 22, 23

horsepower, 9
hub-centered steering, 11

Integrated Detection Systems (BIDS), 27

Kevlar, 18, 19

Oldsmobile Jetfire, 7
omnidirectional wheels, 11

radar, 12, 13
rocket cars, 8–9

self-driving cars, 22–23
Siri, 24
smoke screens, 28, 29
spike strips, 28
Spirit of Berlin, 23
stealth fighter jets, 12, 13
SYNC, 25

Terrafugia Transition, 17
Tesi 3D, 11
ThrustSSC, 8–9
transitioning vehicles, 16–17
turbochargers, 6–7

U.S. president's limo, 19
USS *Nautilus*, 7

voice command systems, 24–25

Waterman Aerobile, 16
weapons detection systems, 26–27

# BATMOBILES
## AND
# BATCYCLES
### *THE ENGINEERING BEHIND BATMAN'S VEHICLES*

No one rules the streets of Gotham City like Batman. His road vehicles are tricked out with rocket boosters, weaponry, and so much more. But Batman is a fictional super hero—none of his gear is real, right? Think again!

Look inside to explore the real-world science and engineering that has inspired the Dark Knight's Batmobile and Batcycle.

## BATMAN *SCIENCE*

When it comes to fighting crime, technology is Batman's greatest weapon. From his gadget-packed Utility Belt to his high-tech Batmobile, the Dark Knight tackles Gotham City's criminal underworld. But does any of his gear have a basis in reality? Or is it merely the stuff of fiction? *Batman Science* explores real-life science and engineering—and their connections to Batman's gear may surprise you.

### TITLES IN THIS SET:

**BATARANGS AND GRAPNELS:**
THE SCIENCE BEHIND BATMAN'S UTILITY BELT

**BATMOBILES AND BATCYCLES:**
THE ENGINEERING BEHIND BATMAN'S VEHICLES

**BATPLANES AND BATCOPTERS:**
THE ENGINEERING BEHIND BATMAN'S WINGS

**BATSUITS AND CAPES:**
THE SCIENCE BEHIND BATMAN'S BODY ARMOR

## Capstone Press®
a capstone imprint    www.capstonepub.com

RL: 3-4  IL: 5-9

ISBN 978-1-4765-5208-8

90000

9 781476 552088